One World
of Poetry

One World of Poetry

BY

THE POET AMIN

www.bookstandpublishing.com

Published by
Bookstand Publishing
Morgan Hill, CA 95037
4708_8

ISBN 978-1-63498-826-1

Back Cover Art Photo
Larry Jackson aka Mr. Data

(R.I.P. John Boyd)

Printed in the United States of America

In loving memory of

My brother Keith Clayton (Jazil)

"What goes around comes around I figga
Now we got white kids calling themselves niggas
The tables' Turrrrrn, as the crosses burrrrrn
Remember you, must, learrrrn
About the styles I flip, and how wild I get
I go on like a space age rocket ship"

KRS ONE (Metaphysician)

This book is dedicated to

my father, Thomas Hill
and step mother, Novellar Hill

My Thanks

First and for most, God
I know without faith in my Higher Power
None of this would be possible
Also my best friend (Mother)
Love you always and forever
My step father (Larry Owens) for his words of wisdom
Charles Mullins for aiding me through the steps of recovery.
Wishing everyone who is a fan of the arts, peace and blessings.

RED BLACK & GREEN WISDOM

Table of Contents

Introduction

One world of poetry is like a stick of dynamite
About to explode into a million little pieces
That can be sorted into a beautiful puzzle
So people can see its design sparkling like glitter
Within the deep darkness of the world today
I wrote these poems in 2005

Most of them were full with a lot of hate and anger
But since I have been living in recovery
And enjoying life today for the most part, my visions have changed
So what I did was bring more life and light to them
Some poems were very wordy and on the lame side.
But back in 05 I thought they were really hitting on something

Now I see why other poets kept telling me to keep writing! Haha
These were also my days of active addiction
And major depression at large, so what I did was keep the titles
and added some meat to this stew of poems cooked well done
This book was actually supposed to come out
Before Life Hell & Heaven

but since Life Hell & Heaven is the story of my life
in a poetry format, I thought that needed to be published first
plus, KRS taught me, "if you don't know the history of the author
then you don't know what you are reading"
I call this book One World of Poetry for several reasons
One, the art pieces deal with one frame of mindset 'Poetry'

Circulating around many causes and effects
Connecting to many levels of light sources combine as One.
Two, they were created as I was battling dark thoughts
Trying to find my place in society which led me to
The Poet writers' galaxy of artist Heaven, so these are the poem
manifestations of ideas conceived during that travel.

This book deals with one truth about the ups and downs of the soul
Taking control of the artist world trying to seek balance
To complete his mission as a Poet, and at the last minute
I decided to make the book two parts because more was revealed
To me from a Higher state of consciousness in its final touch up
I hope you enjoy it and find it helpful in stressful situations

That life may bring your way, and on that note
like my man Ced G of 'Ultramagnatic MC's' said
"here I go, here I go, and here I go again!"

Part One

Sword of Power

Brain Operation

4 3 2 1 dark clouds covered the bright sun
Now the whole world will be stung by this scorpion
War is like evil it will never be done
And that's only because no one has ever won
Watching them all run toward the light sound that the Poet sung
Being attacked by my nephews and their water guns

Picture the writer being scared of a polar bear
The brain is always aware but sometimes unprepared
I wander and roam through the danger zones
Another zig zag ziggila for my annex of poems
Like a computer I shall type exploring at new heights
Your first lesson was wrong so let's try to make it right

I moved a rock with my mind using a little bit of my might
So if I was to do what not I still wouldn't give up the fight
Now can we listen to Babyface on this Saturday night?
Like KRS said, "we bring the liiiiiiiiiiiiight!!!!!"
The sun beams down on an open stream
You know the one that flows like the poetry of Amin

Words I speak be like ocean deep
Life is a mountain and I am trying to climb up to the highest peek
Soon I will be in a movie scene just liked I always dreamed
Getting rid of anything dirty you can call me Mr. Clean
A Poet master don't mean to flatter
But these poems of mine have been thought of as quite spectacular

And be sure not to miss out on a poetry twist
The brain operation is marvelous
Out to bend anything that's straight
As I continue to write poetry without taking breaks
And best believe my third eye sees what's going on
All around the world hearing the same old song

Your whole career has been veneer
Just like the United States governors and mayors
There will be no more fishing and lots of tension
If the art committees were to come with poetry restrictions
With what is known as dereliction
It's the brain operating when our love for the arts collide

But if the authorities were here I most likely would defy
The stories in my last book stated were mostly R rated
I never been gang related just alienated
Being a loser to drugs could be a possibility
Some people be overwhelmed by my conformity
I show appreciation for friends' like Brian, Derrick, and Terrence

We give each other relief with our own adherence
So whatever the Canaanites are giving we're not having it
As your speeches seem to be more and more inadequate
Life is already rough you have done enough
Can you imagine something being said without a must
Leaders follow leaders now haven't you seen her

Sentencing poets to life for misdemeanors
What it means is that I can be jailed for this
But whatever the case I will not languish
These are thoughts trapped inside my mental
Knowing that there is more than one dogma for masses of people
Nobody's invincible to death which coincides with life

And the foundation of any spiritual principles
Rather it's coming from The Poet Amin or Sir Venerable
And what's life without sex? I'm feeling more complex
Destroying and building as they prepare for what's next
Coming from my love for the arts and opposite attraction
Practicing painting pictures filled with words of abstraction

Plain Truth

Now I hope everyone is ready because this Poet comes heavy
Even if the powers that be won't let me
But those with closed minds won't be ready for this one
And that's only because their lacking common sense and wisdom
But some devil worshipers are beginning to worship God
Because the light of the poetry has gotten in them

Everyone can have ever lasting life
As long as you have faith in what is right
Dancing in the brightness of the sun shining at night
Is not the way you were taught trying to connect thoughts
Because it has been all kinds of messages brought
Through the word play mixture that's nice like beans and rice

Quality time and concentration makes a poem come out hype
Who cares if the whole world knows my down falls
It's a total eclipse of the heart craving for cocaine and alcohol
I remember waking up crying there's no sense in lying
The disease of addiction had my whole life on pause
So whatever came out of my mouth was guaranteed false

Every day being ungrateful and expressing pain
Knowing if I can become positive and strong
I would be on top of my art game
Taking the road less traveled in search of fame
Times in recovery can be rough but we gotta be tough
Remaining drug and alcohol free no matter what

Even when we are feeling like lonely creampuffs
And now that I am finally clean, my life has gotten better
And soon I'll have a book full of love letters
Getting a little loose tasting the Poet's heavenlicious juice
Dealing with the facts of the matter by writing down plain truths

Laws of Nature

The laws of nature may seem ungodly
But it's not our universal Mother and Father
That's destroying everybody
If you want peace we gotta strive for peace
Only love will destroy this evil beast
Imagine crime and drugs being out of our existence

Eliminating this fog of ignorance
That travels over us like some kind of curse
Quenching men thirst making matters worse
So no matter what I must keep God first
A lot of helpful insight gets buried alive
But thanks to the wise for making the dead rise

Like myself and others to all my sisters and brothers
I was never a fighter I've always been an amazing lover
of this beautiful world, it's one of Gods' precious pearls
That's why the laws of life man try to observe
Overall I'm grateful refusing to walk around being hateful
And remember it was a love thought that made you

Swimming in an ocean of endless bliss
The way our beautiful mothers have insist
So I truly believe that I deserve a kiss
of Her after life, not only once but twice
Meditation of the day went very nice
I believe my job as a Poet is to share truth with them

Because I love Her and I'll say it again and again
Doing my best to keep away from returning back to drug addiction
Listening to the Goddess of Wisdom expressing freedom
and I know at the end we all going have to face ya
Yeah it's just the ways of the world or the laws of nature

Shield of Love
(for my beautiful mother)

Every time I look up in the sky I see your face
Every time I close my eyes
I see God's Light shining within your smile
When it is time for prayer I always scream out Mother
When I was in the darkness you were my vision of light
Connected to my soul and spirit

When the demons had me captured, your love ran them away
Now all enemies must die because Momma don't raise no punk
I will forever be loving you more than words can express
Because you were the One with the Source
Before everything and nothing
Creating stars for all to see the motion of one world of poetry

A Heaven for the children and a great great grandmother!
For those living and yet to be born, the one and only natural entity
The most beautiful of the world, our Holy Mother, Mommaboutcha
I have literally seen your Father Lord God holding ya

Poetry Talks

Bodies that died on the street were drawn out in white chalk
Danger swooped down on them and flew away like a hawk
Communities are screaming it is the government's fault
Like a thief that steals but never gets caught
Like the incident that took place out in the heavy thick fog
Reporters on the news were saying it was an inside job

People are starting to investigate Charles Schwaab
Bank of America somehow got robbed
There are thousands of troubles in the parking lot
That people wish they can pass but they stop and shop
Like at the ending of the year we watch the ball drop
What I would like to do is leave you all in shock

That's very possible and I would if I could
But regardless I must remain creative like a Poet should
No I'm not a professor so I'm not here to teach
or a priest so you won't hear me preach
But I can be aggravating like a blood sucking leach
If poetry was England, I'd be the king

But since it's a world of freedom, I'm The Poet Amin
And the color of my flag is red black and green
Now at the very beginning of humanity's creation
It was man and woman not separation
Lies took off like an eagle stalks
But this truth is no longer hidden because of poetry talks

I was surrounded by greed when I planted these seeds
A Poet's job is never done so don't be expecting me to leave
I'm here to give One-Self everything on the shelf
And since I can't do it alone I'm hoping others will help
Now I'm mesmerized by the lady in black
Not trying to get off the subject but baby got back

If you would like to talk about poems on an individual basis
Just keep in mind that I have stacks
That is attacking all wrongs like the attacks on Iraq
If you're addicted to drugs we can even talk about that
And if you think you have been winning by succeeding
Then you better not roll craps

Minds are starting to open up to the messages poems have brought
Whether its love or hate, we still need to remember that poetry talks

Revolution of the Mind

These wonderful artist worlds are the largest
Poetry travels far and it's hard to tell which star
is the farthest away from you sticking on like glue
Letting light shine through our souls and spirits too
Now what the Poet has craft is built to last
As we continue to create several poems from one rough draft

This writer's creative instincts are becoming more persistent
Brilliantly significant like an unending existence
Automation ostentation brain operation as an occupation
Executing a plan for the problems our society are facing
While steady embracing lost souls in God's nation
Looking at the beautiful snow flurries as the mind inquiries

On how not to live without fear and worry
Especially when the disease of addiction was burying me
Alive everyday bravely and had my vision about life blurry
See no one was there when I walked on water
Not to mention how I believed drugs had made me smarter
When they actually made everything about life harder

Disrespecting my mother and poor step father
All throughout the day my soul felt gloomy
So I would become intoxicated and act rudely
Running around with a heartless crew
I had no clue that my life was through
Until I got on this path of a chosen few

Who's taking their time showing me what not to do
In order to remain living a recovery life and above all of you
Demons and devils trying to switch up levels
and hoping to one-day silence this poetry rebel
Which could be dangerous because people are dying
What brings about nights of the Giant Lion?

And more damage would have continued if God did not stop me
Making me forever a member of the steady rock posse
From 1986 to 1990, I really tried my best to deliver poems lightly
Now that's a line taking from my Life, Hell & Heaven design
As we prepare for Armageddon poetry revolution of the mind

Written By

Before we start you really need to know that
Everything you are reading was written by the Poet
These words are like wind moving the trees
Sitting next to a body of water enjoying the cool breeze
Because the direction of the sun is where I'm coming from
That would make these poems sacred and its meat cooked well done

I used to be a street hanger somewhat like a petty drug slinger
Now writing poetry is how I deal with anger
The essence of these writings are filled with abnormal creations
Going way beyond the world's technology with my brain operation
No more smoking cigarettes or trapped by time and space
One of the poisons that can stop me from shocking this place

Creating fate to contemplate causes grounds to shake
Crying streams of rivers making ponds and lakes
Because both of my heads hold a lot of unnecessary weight
And it's still nothing but the truth that I indoctrinate
That some people wish to emasculate but most poets consolidate
Lions and tigers and bears oh myyyyyyy

This is a public service announcement brought to you and written by
The Poet master or rhyme creator
Remaining truthful and real watching others get faker
Free association is very relative, thanks to my heavenly heritage
Speaking a godly language with the words I write or say
and this is a love that shall never fade away

Because where not dealing with lust whatsoever
Which is quite clever standing on the rock in stormy weather
Having fun trying to reach the young, and wipe out damages done
To the soul mind and spirit but there is still no need to fear it
Because those kind of people just grim and berate
Life is a gift that was giving to us so why should we hate it?

The devil enters our heart and tries to make us debate it
And this has nothing to do with anyone considered a racist
Because this savage beast of a man terrorizes all places
Just go back in history and study the cases
It could be seen as a real evil force, that kills with no remorse
Read 'William Cooper's' "Behold A Pale Horse"

Or "New Dimensions in African History" and you'll see clearly
How life is not a mystery, reading materials like "The Peopling of
Ancient Egypt and The Deciphering of the Merotic Script"
Just touching on some of the issues that I'll be coming forth with
When creating poetry confronting Lucifer's Hench-man
Because the nature of evil we should understand

Coming indisputable as I flow so free
and when this death happens to come to me
A casket or box really will not be suitable
So I'm preferring cremation for more gradation
That I hope will place me back right where I need to be
Which is inside of a mental ward pacing back and forth

Waiting to hear another public service announcement
From the thinking machine brought to you and written by
Tarik as his true Self or Higher Visions of The Poet Amin

Divine Inspiration

As we lay down to sleep and prepare ourselves
For what we believe to be another day on God's earth
We become unconscious to life and blind to the darkness
As our spirits move toward '*A Night of the Sun*'
All the great poets will continue to fill up the moon
and soon Captain America will meet Doctor Doom

We all must pay for this evil curse
That was cast down from the heavens to roam among us
A demonic god gathered up an army to go against humanity
The results are blood baths on innocent people's paths
Experimenting on black garbage and white trash
Followers of many soldier dogs, are individuals lost in the fog

of ignorance perseverance taking place since this beast landed
or more like created to preserve all the wisdom that has faded
But still some swim upstream to a world of beautiful dreams
Where we can see ourselves as wonderful kings and queens
Building with angels and Goddesses when we rest at night
That's always our universal selves taking flight

Everything about love is good and its light is always bright
With faith we don't have to fight this evil that man do
Because believe it or not I have always seen you as being untrue
Just like those monster dragon beast wearing blue
Trying to have me believing in something deceiving
Shaking the hands of demons became very misleading

This message will be ever so clear in a recovery meeting
But how can people call themselves spiritual beings
When they can't even come out to support a poetry reading
And this creation expansion is part of my brain operation
or the causes and effects of our worldly rotation
Pass down from generation through divine inspiration

Higher Learning

These so called controllers are trying to control my gift
By wanting me to write with more imitativeness
Imagine your thoughts tied into a knot tightly
In no time I design from the mind with immaculacy
There are many ways to describe how one masculinize
The characteristics of a poem as on an amusement ride

Put your hands up in the sky somebody has stolen the bribe
And threatening to internationalize
If she's the schoolteacher poets have some mercy
Just read his book we already know she's not worthy
Now haven't we had ya sucking blood like Count Dracula
Writers and readers who know this are sitting back laughing at ya

Like a deejay scratching the turn tables turning
We should start in elementary school aiming for a higher learning
Every mind is a victim of this beast system's evil polluting
This is all reflected in the sealed and the constitution
Yes this is an original copy of every hater that mocks me
Which has been done through depth psychology

A clearer demonstration is in position to stress the point or meaning
Because the subject matter can come across as being difficult
or an inconvenience process of thought warned by the black hawk
So whatever this poem brings is not my fault
A permanent pressing I reckon the spiritual world is testing
So higher learning will be today's lesson

It's like vice grips and pliers I have the whole entire script
of these dimensions like episodes of sliders
Love is the most ultimate and it can even be borrowed
When feeling or expressing any emotional sorrow
Just by reframing from any unnecessary quarrels
See these manifestations are filled with admiration

And constant persuasion manipulating the equation
of a sentence fragment, hidden within all this poetry magic
Eliminating negative visions with more positive habits
So hear the writers come full of life and fun
You can close your eyes and still see the light of the sun
Shining on this dark world and within spirits too

Across the seas is where the love birds flew
Walking through the shadow of death accepting all one has left
Accelerating on a higher level keeping the mind fresh
and at bay focusing just on the day that is present
is something that will always be revenant
Returning time after time gaining common sense

When looking around seeing caution signs of warning
Some people don't want our children to enter into a higher learning

Knowledge Is Power

Oh Mother, oh Father, oh Sister, oh Brother,
Oh Aunties, oh Nephews, oh Nieces, oh Cousins...
We have been producing by the dozens
With a lot of history like the city of New London
Now there once was a lion locked inside a cage
But when he was let loose they felt the Poet's rage

At the same time he took it back to his roots
Now I have the recipe for a delicious poetry soup
I was enjoying what you are reading as I sat up on the roof
Destroying facts that people stated without producing proof
Plus if it's not natural it can't be cultural
or compared with one another like the pig and the vulture

An unknown soldier is moving up in ranks
Shooting apples and bananas from out of his tank
To the persons removing love for hate
Now their hearts are hard like the prison bar gates
Let's take a quick break and wait for those who maybe late
And that's just enough time for you to sip on this chocolate shake

So remain calm as I drop the bomb of peace
But keep the dogs on the leash
And hear everyone singing like in the movie *Grease*
Because what the world needs is more happiness
And those who have it are refusing to give
and that makes me despondent

As they became part of the dead beef I ate
It was like feeding a dog a raw steak
This trash pollution they started killed all the fish in the lake
And now they have the nerve to say the whole area stinks
So bad when you come you might drop and faint
But all this is subject to change after reading the poems created

Even though most people might repudiate it
Basically what I'm saying can go on without any acknowledgement
Burning candles around a table sharing truth about accomplishments
Knowledge of self can give an individual freedom
I would love to live a long life expressing Her wisdom
Peace and happiness were born within

And if you look deeply into the eyes you can actually see them
Going blank totally in a blur as they purposely ignore
Anyone that chooses to speak about our Father Lord
That's backing you while keeping our souls beautiful
So it's very important to keep moving right ahead
and at the same time learning how to know the ledge

Because so many people jump over the edge
There will be no god men left if in darkness we rest
Only because ignorance is death
A Poet's job is to spread fun turning sad times into happy ones
So feel free to come and stare at the flaming Sun
And bear witness to everything that's being done

Feeling good as if we were taking a bath or shower
God is truth and Her knowledge is power

The Fog of Ignorance

I was pumping gas when I heard the loud blast
Innocent people murdered for some quick cash
Now were they really innocent or is this the fog of ignorance?
Even if it is we still have to live with it
A Poet cannot make what is fake real
A place and people were just destroyed and killed

and now the authorities want to know who is going to pay the bill
Some use sex appeal to get their thrills
But I'm just a student of the class not the king of the hill
And I refuse to live with this pain for the rest of my life
Having to dig deep inside could cause all kinds of strife
And it is more than just me paying the price

That's why it is important for all gods to unite
Dealing with truth, sharing it with our wonderful youth
Rebuilding a nation full of poetry troops
With a variety of flavors that I'll be serving to you in scoops
Coming equipped always legit wanting to see you become love sick
Overstanding all the wrongs being addressed within this manuscript

It has taking lots of time for a sound and clear mind
Standing behind enemy lines blind to the signs of a bright shine
This fog of ignorance swallowed my years of prime

Life Is Short

The beginning is the ending because life is short
Transmitting while you are sipping on the poems I transport
In the woods I built a shack and called it God's fort
The principle is dispensable reciting riddles while I fondle and fiddle
The plug in the socket before I take off like a rocket
Into space leaving behind no trace with pen and paper just in case

The center of my brain strained while feeling somewhat strange
Screaming more change for the same while expressing pain
and the womb of the universe makes sure it continues to rain
Beneath the astral plane of a conscious high
Multiply by the sun, moon, and stars in the sky
Putting everything aside for another poetry ride

Moving in like water from the ocean tide
No need to be worried, I made sure it was done with effrontery
And maybe an arrogant assumption about nothing for something
If I have love in my life than what else is that I'm wanting?
That would probably be leaving my poetry fans in shock
Literally as if their heart beats stopped

Remaining coming in from over the top
Scoring a touchdown every time the ball is caught
Striving to be seen as one with God's team
The Reverend Martin Luther had a beautiful dream
Yeah I know it sounds too good to be true so it must be a scheme
I must acknowledge all that is blurry with observatory

Thinking I will be writing at seventy because of longevity
So please let me come inside that would be so soothing
It's the works of a Poet operating smooth and
As I designed from the mind like Albert Einstein
But not a close encounter of a third kind
Strictly original with these art material visuals

As if I have been around since the beginning of people
Reciting poems about a life unsung or untyped
Telling you about the criminals that were sacrifice with Christ
Who happen to also be gods holding the sword of power and light
And once again the laws put an ending to that fight
I am telling you this so you can walk through the cloudy mist

Plus you can't score a touchdown trying to catch the ball and miss
That's why I choose to stay religious isolationist
I read about the land origin of the major western blanks
And learned that all the answers are in museums and banks
This music funk is starting to smell like somebody stinks
So off we dip into a bucket of paint

Tomb stones shine like chrome within my annex of poems
I gave her a beautiful baby but now she leaves me alone
I guess Mama was right I should have stayed at home
Our love travels so far we left behind two clones
On the run like slaves hiding out in caves
Somebody else had to become rich because I never got paid

But that's okay because I perfected the trade
And it brought more than one person better days
My reward is bliss she gave me a kiss for that
That's one hundred million years better then smoking crack
"Is that the number one Poet" now why would you ask that?
of course it is, I'll break a struggle with a miracle like Joe Morris

I have been doing what I am doing when it comes to art assiduously
Ever since drugs built a self-made prison for me
Swallowing my pride showed that my character was bigger
Then those black folks down south who called me a proper nigger
Could it be true the slave masters up north treated us better than you
Some were taught how to read and write and that's very cool

The way I see it there is just a lot of poor sports
Flashing back to the beginning of our ending because life is short

I Can't Get Up

I was zoomed in up close as I sat still in a dark corner
My back against the wall, my mind was in a whirlpool
Twirling inside a triangle as I reached for a light
Seeing my mother's face as the lighter flicks on
My father was the roach crawling across the floor
Waving bye to me, I stuck up my middle finger

As a tear fell from my left eye
Reminiscing about my days of elementary
I always felt handicapped when I had to use my brain for anything
At the same time, I was building an imaginary world within my mind
My mother used to say If she had money she'd send me for counseling
Sometimes I think if that would have helped me find direction

I should have learned something from all my childhood lessons
I probably wouldn't be sitting in this corner stressing
At a young age my destiny was to die on the streets
So I'm very upset about hearing my heart beat
The lighter flicks again because I am just that weak
I need to start doing some push-ups tomorrow and read a book too

My Pop's came back in a mouse form to say hi and see how I was
This time I stuck both my middle fingers up
As a tear felled from my right eye, banging my head against the wall
Shadows appeared, my heart is beating faster, but I'm not scared
Hoping these demons take me away and throw me in the fire pit
Before I hurt another innocent soul, but all they did was jack me up

Like the police usually do and left me too rot in this corner
So now I'm looking at the light shining from under the door
Down to my last hit and I want some more, the lighter flicks again
I hear my Mother saying get away from me fool
The whole town is calling me a druggie
As I start to think about my nephews wanting to be rebels

But the spiritual ugly will never rest in peace
I never should have befriended the voodoo priest
Yes I attended meetings amongst devils and demons
When I was a hardcore drug addict on the streets scheming
But now all the drugs are gone, and I will do anything for more
But I cannot seem to get up from off of this floor

Stuck in this dark corner, my dad appeared again in a rat form
To see if I made any achievements in my life
I wanted to punch him but I just couldn't
Tears were rolling down from both eyes and I can see everyone else
Who was concerned praying for me, as they stood in back of him
There had to be at least twelve to fifteen rats
And all I can say was "can yal not see that I can't get up?"

"No disrespect to my dad whatsoever
Because I have a wonderful Father
Love you Pop's."

Who's There

I must have been asleep when all this took place
One may ask, when what took place?
And I will answer them by saying "my life as it is"
First of all, what happened to my strength
Where is the power I thought I had, "It's hidden in the dark"
Is what the voice of my shadow shouted out

So now I think I need a flashlight, and my eyes checked
Because those qualities are very important
As I walk through the land of wilderness
Sometimes it feels as if my mind has been draggled
And sometimes the voices of my shadow comes out of my mouth
And nobody knows what I am talking about

So I am just going to continue running, not from my troubles
But to a place of emptiness, no responsibilities, no air to breathe,
and no longer me, just life elements remaining
Awww man, here comes that evil entity laughing at me
Thinking I am copping a plea, so maybe I'll clean up the outside
Then my enemies might think the inside is clean as well

But I still cannot escape the shadow of death, and this is proof
of it being more than one war going on inside my little mind
So what am I to do? Space and time is not helping
Alcohol and drugs are not helping, knowledge of self is not helping
When I try to keep busy, visions of being a failure comes into play
Slowing me down or just making me stop trying to achieve goals

Just turning corners over there, and turning corners over here
If it's not a continuous pathway, then it must be a dead end
So it looks like I have to make my own way on someone else's path
Who is probably no longer here, plus I like traveling alone
Not caring what others think about me being confused
Hey wait a minute, that looks like me over there

Yeah over there smoking cigarettes right before class
Nah wait a minute, that might be me over there
With those drug addicts getting high, nah that can't be me
That might be me over there in that nice car
With that hot foxy momma, nah wait a minute
just wait one damn minute because that's not me

I think that's me over there studying for my diploma
And that can be me graduating too, nah wait a minute
That can't be me over there making all those people laugh and smile
Nah wait a minute, that can't be me over there in that casket
Lying in the back of someone church's funeral home
What is the best way to prepare for these kind of spiritual wars?

I don't know, but this unconscious state of mind may last forever
So now I lay me down to sleep, I pray the Lord my soul to keep
and if I should die before I wake, I pray the Lord my soul to take
Knock knock, "who's there?" Me! "Wait a minute"
knock knock, "who's there?" Me! "Me who?"
You? "Oh me?" No not you stupid, me!

"Nah, hold on and just wait one minute"
No sir, a minute is too much time to waste
"Okay, well can you just tell me who's in here/there?"

Two Me(s)
(Inspired by my cousin Marco Maddox)

The power of poetry expresses two me(s)
One is locked in a room, one walks around free
One is in control, but one doesn't know
One be moving too fast, and one be moving too slow
There's really nothing like a poetry show
Even though I was hit with a real low blow

It made me lose my breath, it made me stop my flow
Why she do it? I really don't know!
I was looking for the door that led to the back
Right before the magician pulled the cat from out of the hat
And that made me realize that this lonely bird shall fly
The truth can't hurt me, so there is no need to hide

It was a lesson learned so I waited for my turn
Watching my mind travel like smoke every time fire burns
Nobody has won as much as my poetry firm
But that's temporary like a woman's perm
I won't act conceited like no one can beat it
But the little goals I have set has already been completed

I still have your letter but never read it
Like God is coming you'll be waiting to see it
Now I'm interrupted by one of me(s)
One will do it for a fee; one will do it for free
Like karate's Bruce Lee had the highest degree
One travels lightly, one thinks he's almighty

One tries to stay high that's one that's low
One tries to stay positive that's the one that's slow
When one tries to stop the other one always go
One was offered drugs by a scarecrow
My mouth said yes but the God within said no
When one forgets, one will let me know

That one is Muslim, one is Christian
One pays attention, one won't listen
Continue the mission, my intuition
and if you can't stand the heat, stay out of the Poet's kitchen
When writers come up or down, I come sideways
Death is a dead end, life is a highway

There's a beautiful waitress that works at Fridays
But I wish it was Burger King so I could have it my way
One me thought of change, the other me said me too
Because I really don't know what else to do
One me be showing the other me flaws in my poetry
One is real, one is phony, the blind is holding me lost and lonely

So may I please continue to watch the wind blow the trees
Two me(s) together is like macaroni and cheese
I knew a guy named Kindu who used to love Nintendo
And there was never any kind of meat on his food menu
A pretty young lady drove me crazy
I was like a pencil on her paper because she tried to erase me

It's like the 12 Jewels of Islam, or the 10 Buddhist Gems of life
Two me(s) will fight, wrong or right?
Let's hope neither one of us loses sight
We'll be extinct like dinosaurs, earth's final war
You and I will be no more

Human Webs (here comes the spider)

Who feels like going hunting for man?
The man and woman who are caught up inside human webs
These unnecessary blood baths turned the waters red
I searched and found things written by the dead
Now imagine a dumpster filled with heads
Others are starting to look into some things I said

Well keep in mind that I'm going crazy, and I stopped taking meds
So please don't push me because I'm close to the edge
There used to be two me(s) but now there are ten
Running wild blowing hard in the wind
This is only a poetry twist, not a world of sin
The language of imagination strikes again

This story won't become hazy for personal reasons
What are you doing around here lady?
don't you know it's man season? A time to kill evilness for real
Just stay away from that house on the hill
I feel like I just rolled over in a puddle of rain
Hoping I can help someone by expressing pain

These could be the characteristics of a poetry militant
Trapped in a world of confusion and ignorance
We started off in a puddle but now we're in a bloody pond
How can drugs destroy the poetry Don?
Well it's quite easy because it grabs me and squeezes me
But the God of my understanding came to free me

And Her loving was good she made me tired
My job is to inspire now here comes the spider
The angel of death shall put me to rest
So one of me(s) is gone and there are nine left
Well what do we know while observing the pretty white snow
Or the greatest entertainer in a poetry show

Mother Nature is beautiful but not Her storms
You can't escape your fate, the whole world was warned
So honk like a truck's horn, it's the early bird that gets the first worm
The worm seems to be my evil that's taking me higher
Ah man here comes the spider, the angel of death took me away
Because one of these days will be none of these days

I got hit by a stray in a screenplay
You really should be hearing what the Poet has to say
I freed myself from the pond but now I'm trapped in a lake
There was nine of me(s) but now there is only eight
Most of us walk sideways when we should be walking straight
Filled with so much pain got me feeling a little shameful

These kind of thoughts alone can be very painful
And now I hear you want to fire your most creative writer
God bless me because here comes the spider
The angel of death ripped my heart from out of my chest
When I was smoking crack I should have been smoking sass
Now I'll find out for sure if there is a hell or heaven

There were eight me(s) but now there are seven
Where's Mommy and Daddy my little brother's telling
That he saw her mouth on my stick, I had no choice but to lick
We were in that love position when you both can feel it
But now it's back to the streets for a life of crime
This stereo player only has forward there is no rewind

Sometimes I think of me being conceived as a waste of time
The only thing I remember is the wicked witch
Here comes the spider of death again so now there is only six
Of Me(s) hiding out in the trees
These are just poetry tales and you can do whatever you please
So I don't want to hear God bless you if I was to sneeze

Yes I have an attitude because I am caught up in the web alright
But here comes a different spider, this is the angel of life
See half of me died, the other half is still alive
This story started out with ten but now we are down to five
In this land of wilderness only the strong survives
Oh my I am hearing cries the Poet was found dead on the floor

God took him away so now there is only four Me(s)
Chopping up wood surviving as best we could
So understand this life lesson and receive your blessing
How many times do I need to say know the ledge and stop guessing
Maybe many more times until I am set free
Here's double the money that the devil lent me

I am like a car that's low on fuel and you're gassing me
Without acknowledging the Poet's creativity
I would like to be caught up in a web of peace
But here comes that spider so now there are three
What else can I do to be able to get on through
The spider must have come because I am only seeing two left

Fighting for breath wishing we had cleaned up our bird's nest
A writer's job will never end, and poets don't retire
Everyday someone dies as life becomes livelier
Now what we are dealing with is a total of *two Me*(s)
Damn!! And here come two spiders

A Killer's on the Loose

Here it is wee hours in the morning and I can't even close my eyes
It's not because I am depressed, well maybe a little
But this cough is killing me; lately I've been smoking cigarettes
using hardcore drugs, walking around with a dangerous weapon
And running from God's love, trying to sum things up quick
Because my poems seem to always be so long

The enemy was once my weak side that became so strong
From the days of kindergarten, I have been mistreated
And now it seems like everybody be telling me to beat it
That's why I kept going outside when I should have stayed inside
A lady friend laid her head on my chess
and said she heard my heart crying

Hearing voices say kill yourself, kill yourself, not really wanting
To be a victim of another death by suicide
And for those who may try to destroy my works
Will most likely end up dead, if not just getting physically hurt
Everyone has a dark side, I know about seven unsolved homicides
Remembering those who have lied, running but can never hide

This truth that leads to power refinement
Going from being self-righteous to open-minded
Here's my letter to the authorities yes the doctor signed it
I was feeling spiritually sick and mentally blinded
But now I am used to traveling through these dark skies
Death is the number one killer and we all are going to die

Death after Life

Ladies and gentlemen
I come to you with creativity
It's The Poet Amin VS Tarik C.
The world took its last breath as the people left
You either live your life or die along with death
When a person dies they have only awaking

When a person lives they have only falling asleep
And since this is the case, I may have died last week
Some people souls can be dead spiritually
Only to hopefully someday live
And civilize the blind like Moses did
You know the death, dumb, and blind individuals like myself

So first the handle will be fix and then whatever else
I started asking for help from God after I destroyed my health
She whispered pick out the most spiritual book on the shelf
But they were all religionize and couldn't be felt
So I had no choice but to play with the cards I was dealt
So beware of the things you are doing and keep in mind whose ruling

Because poetry will stay in motion like the earth is always moving
Tarik means the comer of light
and sometimes you can see me shinning from a far
And if you don't understand what I'm saying
I am basically telling you that I am like a piercing star
Believing in myths doesn't take away from our God giving gifts

Some have died never knowing what their names meant
Stepping into a world of the airy element
Keeping up with our own pace while floating in space
Here we will see other cultures categories as part of the human race
So see why I call this poem death after life?
Beautiful plus Blackness equals Bright

My father met a beautiful woman in 1970
and since my father is a wise man, the connection was heavenly
In within the next five years he planted two seeds
So even before I was conceived I was meant to lead
It took 22 years before I learned how to read
But as Amin or Tarik, poetry was still achieved

Snakes in the grass would see me coming and leave
Because my presence alone made it hard for them to breathe
So don't be afraid to drop down to your knees
And ask God directly to help you succeed
Even back in the days when I couldn't read or write
People still wanted to hear my flow on the mic

That's why I will always represent SRP to the end
Every poem I created was written down by friends
So see why I am calling this poem death after life?
Because people are dying while believing the hype
But I have been riling in my people like a fishing rod
Those who jumped in the pool as niggers but came out as gods

From just a glimpse of the light, souls became bright
and a positive way of living is what we now like
This occupation came by transformation and reformulation
Or a society of man and woman building a whole new nation
That makes it a shame for all the evil trying to destroy the Poet
What I've spoken has been quoted the one who wrote it knows it

So can you see why I am calling this poem death after life?
A lot of people are convinced that heaven is nice
The facts arc very little though and highly dispensable
Now if you still don't get the poem try reading it twice
We all must travel through death after life

Light and Dark

Here I am writing a poem on a white sand beach
Trying to escape the words I heard in the preacher's speech
Talking about the light as he held onto the mic
But see a Poet like me is always ready to fight
These inhumane thoughts have done damage to the heart
It's like being locked in a room that is completely dark

And not only is depression making me lazy
But I am starting to feel like I am going crazy
Dropping out of school because I thought that was cool
Seeing it as life be in it like in a swimming pool
At the end of the rainbow they been telling us there is a pot of gold
But what they did not tell us was in order to achieve it

We would have to sell our souls to the driver carrying loads
of this truth, that is so blunt and bold, the world is just too cold
Like a stick of dynamite about to explode
Leading our leaders to the grave site of the Poet buried in a nice suit
But of course after sometime it didn't look so cute
All because you didn't want us to eat the fruit

Seek knowledge and wisdom and become an Earth god like you
And all those checking better keep on stepping
To avoid being a victim of a dangerous weapon
Because what goes around comes around as it is so let it
Returning back to the Garden of Eden walking around naked
So I said to the preacher please give me a break

And he told everyone of the church that I was the snake
See I don't what to continue on full of sin and hate
Flowing downstream unconsciously while awaking
By an intruder with something more super
About the conditions of us human beings in a stupor
Fighting these poisonous insects like starship troopers

Under the orders of a ruler who is also known as Mr. Fooler
Making the people of his team losers and professional verbal abusers
Highly upset about the Poet who has risen from all this thanksgiving
Is how we will see these situations once we get to the ending
of this deep darkness that you will see even better in the light
Looking at the ocean waves as a form of life
Saying to myself "I can't believe this big blue sea has a dark side"

Suicide Jump

I jump off a cliff that was really steep
I had no idea that the water wasn't deep
But before I landed knowledge of God was reached
So everything I give is for you all to keep
You really should try to hear what I'm saying
And do away with all the games people be playing

As we try to eliminate our hate and bring back the love
Because back in the days that's what my poetry was
The highest level of love is understanding, understood
But out of fifteen poets only one was good
When people ignore me it makes me cry
So at twelve years old I started getting high

and it blurred my vision so now the Poet is blind
And so since that's the case I'm letting my darkness shine
Poetry weighs thousands of pounds
And it is our individuality that wears the crown
The sky is big and I want to fly free like a dove
What the children need are more kisses and hugs

I am seeing diamonds and pearls oh what a beautiful world
So can we live and let live boys and girls
Ladies and gentlemen this Poet is telling them
That I wanted my own show like Dave Lettermen
I went from riches to rags, a car to a cab
But this is not a story about what I had

It's about self-destruction and suicide, hellos and goodbyes
She told me to lay down and enjoy the ride, but then she left me
All alone in the bed sheets, and the lonely dies slowly
So can you see why I leaped?
Some people say if you kill yourself you are a chump
But that's not the truth; my mind was just made up

Now that I think about it, everything about this girl was a stunt
But it's too late, because I've already jumped

The Whole World Will Boil

One day when it was hot and sunny
and I needed some money to feed my tummy
And being that my heart is full of hate nobody loves me
So I've been thinking about eliminating the hating
And using my mind for a more positive creation
Like a soda pop having to twist the top

And I wanted to stop because of writer's block
And for tough situations I like to make them soothing
Every time my poetry is in motion like a ship boat costing
I felt like a faggot or a bunch of sticks
The flavor was sweet so I started to lick
A piece of God's Blackness shining just is bright as Her Light

Giving you total truth whenever I pick up a pen and write
You can call me a poetry soldier, or a galaxy protector troop
Getting down to the roots of this forbidden fruit
Following a leader that's a false prophet or teacher
Especially for those of us who are writers and not the reader
See I have a grudge because another man had the nerve to judge

My style of poetry and he never been stab or hit with slugs
And would like for me to sweep all this dirt up under the rug
But you should continue to knock on wood
Especially after being known for wearing the devil's white hood
And if you really love poetry then take the bad with the good
Am like a vulture flying around seeking out the dead world wide

But after it was all said in done it ended up being a waste of time
Because I got trapped in a rap song that was pounded out with bass
And an enemy from the other side remembered my face
So now where at war in this land some call a holy place
And our heavenly Mother and Father think that we are all a disgrace
But who really cares my goal is to control all the earth's oil
And if I can't, the whole world will boil!

I'm Not a Comedian

Welcome to the club's seminar
It's a beautiful scene like looking up at the stars
Poetry is like a sports game and players are scoring points
As hell storms swarm like the road warrior
Every human soul was invaded by evil
Turning the people into little creepy crawlers

Watching all those who are big fall harder
Some say our Lord Father helps those who help themselves
Well that's not fair for the handicap
But united dogs and cats are putting a stop to that
By polluting the rest of the world with rats
What else were you expecting see I'm not a comedian

This is how the fake star that has only been created
To operate evilly trying to darken the minds of everybody
Well the damage has been done working for more than just money
While we are slaving and craving for a little hit becoming richer
To destroy things quicker got poor Mother earth getting sicker
Waiting for a gift to be delivered to have peace like in the beginning

What else were you expecting see I'm not a comedian
Maybe the philosopher can be more lenient
Only if you saw through the eyes of the one that's seeing it
Everyone seem to be stealing and killing by the billions
Too fast to grasp the concept, moral, or meaning
What else were you expecting see I'm not a comedian

Point Blank In Your Face

When the school bell rung I was singing my song
But I said in the beginning that it wouldn't last that long
And everybody was hoping that I was wrong
The competitor was brain damaged from being pound
This poetry fight won't last five rounds
In round three the Poet went down

At the same time other writers acknowledged that the poetry is great
as I left the place, so point blank in your face
I set up in a tree eating bananas, my mind was protected from evil
By wearing a black bandana, enjoying the beautiful sky
Watching the police pass by as they hoped to get one of the monkeys
Into the back of one of their cruisers for a ride downtown-

to the station for cell placement, after a little shock treatment
that takes place in the devil's basement
And there is really nothing we can do but try to walk through
Or run for the gun wanting to know why this has to take place for
Reading books can open up doors, so point blank in your face
I woke up one day in outer space, but not feeling out of place

Because this same kind of ignorance was destroying the alien race
But I have no idea how I woke up in her bed
And people quoting things that I never said
And to make matters worse I am wearing white, blue, and red
All the poets in the ghettos saw my face and fled
Then there were these rumors going around that I went brain dead

Now what was I to do after seeing how some do
People jumping to conclusions without having any clues
I was gaining knowledge of self in a school for fools
Made to wear red white and blue, and that's the god honest truth
But just before I closed the poetry scene
I told them God colors are red, black, and green

So no matter if you ever see me wearing red, white, and blue
I'm still The Poet Amin, so point blank in your face
You may have seen me hanging around down at the poets' lounge
A place some might consider dangerous grounds
If we are responsible for our actions, there is no one to blame
This poetry rebel wars against the devil on any and all levels

Because I am a soldier that cannot let truth end up in just any place
And get away from the human race, so point blank in your face
It is not because the water jammed the beaver's dam
Or the Giant Lion slaughtering the ram
Being watched over by the authorities with a sky cam
For spitting hard truth that goes against Uncle Sam

The goal is to do all I can, after learning the most dangerous weapon-
is an educated black man, so point blank in your face

Part Two

Light of Confusion

Student of the Devil

It was seen as a falling star coming from the dark side
To a people to give them simple star light simple
Because they were cursed for giving birth to evil
Meetings discussing their duty took place inside a cemetery
Rules were laid down with no questions asked
Documents are based on three sequences, liquid, solid, and gas

And if you want to know how I know
It's because in prison I was bless by the gods with math
I'm talking about knowledge, wisdom, and understanding
Not some kind of difficult numerology task
An evil entity resides out in the rivers, and overseas it formed a beast
Always in disguise despising what the Poet teach

Social activities pursuing in the evening
So in the morning you can see them leaving
It's like they are boxing, bobbing, and weaving
It took centuries for them to get even
So many are blind to what these devil worshippers believe in
They know they are doomed for an ending, hiding within religions

It may even look like they are winning, unknown of their beginning
Telling us the story of Cane murdering Abel
But never mentioning how he was paid from under the table
Yes, the money was giving to him by a down man
Working for Satan's military intelligence clan
And if this ain't the truth than I'll be damned

Let's say the poison is actually natural, but scientists made the drugs
You should hear how the poets collaborate walking through mud
I don't have time to answer any questions
I'm about to go further into this lesson
Picture painting God black has caused me to be marked for attack
Considered as a man of the Nile, buried inside the system files

As a Poet guerilla rebel speaking truth about these cold devils
Now the dumb shall be wise, and know who's telling all the lies
Maybe everybody will get invited to this beast master's party
And we can all drink its booze, preparing for our children to lose
After all I'm just a babbling fool, playing around with man's tools
Like animals locked in a zoo being told what to do
So I'm giving my readers a clue, that will be revealed in part two

Sarcasm

In the midst of writing these words, someone look over my shoulder
And witnessed a crime committed by a God Body named Jehovah
Blowing up a federal building for all the people they be getting over
and ever since this hot day, the nights have gotten much colder
and for that I was arrested, for the laws I have disrespected
I never knew these evil individuals and the judge were connected

So in jail I met this man, who had a real clever plan
We broke out of prison and was at it again
Then it just so happened that I saw him doing Jihad
That's when a Muslim Praises God, he had received a message
To destroy all his enemies in the name of Allah
So I contacted the authorities when I figured out his plan

He was out to kill people, mostly the innocent ones of our land
The FBI ignored me, and this poem is starting to bore me
But everyone in the west worlds looked confused
When it was being shown on the news
They so-called blew up the towers, after being trained in our schools
The world was on a standstill, except for the town of Bin Laden field

No need to get upset because what you are reading is not real
When you mess with the red white and blue monsters
It seems like the media acts even dumber
For punishment they sentence me to be crucified
Now I am sitting in a holding cell saying "please, oh my"
And it was my personal Lord and Savior, that was by my side

The listeners called me a criminal, and for a Buddhist that's critical
So I spoke to my personal Lord and Savior
and ask him to perform a miracle? He just said, "Believe in me
and you'll be living eternally" now this might be a mystery
If it goes down in history, see I believe in reincarnation
Alienated by the segregation, if this story ever gets told to the nation

45

It is guaranteed to have religion and scientists debating
All I remember was looking up in the sky
As it rained because our Momma Nature had started to cry
And this fairytale was not a lie
because I watched his soul rise with my own two eyes
and three days later God was seen happily alive
But the Poet had to die

The Poet's Rage

I have been living in a world among a whole lot of strangers
And ready to release some build up anger rather ignorantly
But properly so the outside forces won't be able to stop me
My thought process association is free
Expressing love through creativity describing this city
Or land of the strange staff committee with uniformity

Concerning situations about a Poet's soul that has faded
Back to the womb of the universe finally making it
Scholars from all around the world came and debated
Why a God man or people is considered to be the most hated
Human species, and its conclusion relieved me
Knowing discipline of self will help us grow more spiritually

Keeping the vicious Giant Lion locked in its caged
And freedom from active addiction is the raft of my rage
Manifested live on stage in a poetry plague
For my brother Keith who is in an unmarked grave
New Britain Connecticut is where his physical was laid to rest
As I get some more off my chest sorting through this mess

At a young age I didn't know I was depressed
Never was known as one for holding his breath
Life alone could be one big test
and if you fail not to ever learn this you shouldn't be impress
Born to find a purpose in a world of complete darkness
Where the people are bold and cold and also very heartless

No longer feeling Mother Almighty breeze blowing on me
Realizing I'm still my own worst enemy
Because Simon Says from way back in the days
Malikowski Circle is where I played, trapped in a mental haze
Of delusions blinded by the Light of Confusion
Admitting that I am only one of the people that society has fooling

Sitting back in the shade believing what man has made
Purchasing a product that you would later want to go back and trade
Now I may be coming across vague speaking about the Poet's rage

Student of the Devil (Part Two)

It was seen as a falling star, a lost soul traveling far
Deep into the darkness and soft hearts became hard.
Clouds of evil stay over he choosing to talk about this bluntly
But ever since the devil students' arrived
The universe has been blind
So I believe it is proper to talk about the seven sorcerers.

Creating poems is a habit, delivered as a gift by those who have it
Now the first of the seven sorcerers is a curse called <u>white magic</u>
That has settled around the world in many places
Looking sick with ugly on their faces, but truth connect all races.
<u>White magic</u> is nothing more or less
Than invoking spirits, or evil spirits, and demons in the flesh.

Now let's move right along to the second
That I'll be expressing in a matter of seconds
A savage magnet face I'll rag it, while destroying something
or anything a person loves is considered <u>gray magic</u>.
Now let's move right along to the third
It's hard to make it clear when trying to rhyme words

So the goal is to avoid disasters that tarnishes skills of a Poet master
And hear a wicked man's laughter, but this rage raddles the cage
Especially when talking about <u>black magic</u> after being laid
To bring about total destruction on a person's evil ways.
Now let's move right along to the fourth
With the headless man riding around necked on a horse, <u>red magic</u>

Is one daring with no feelings of caring invoking the Luciferians.
Now let's move right along to the fifth
I feel like bringing forth a poetry twist
But I can't cause that would stink in move me down the ranks
in the middle of a poem like this. The <u>imitative</u> sorcerer
uses pictures or paintings illustrating something

they wish to happen by magic and invoking that instance to occur.
Now let's move it right along to the sixth
Like a stream of water flowing quick
The contagious tale is when one can cast a spell
on an enemy by stealing a piece of hair or fingernail
and turn your life into a living hell.

I don't really know where this poem is headed
But number seven is sympathetic
This means to bewitch or kill the sorcerer
That would make a time model of the person and burn it
or stick pins in it as ordered by the wicked witch.
Now if you know what I'm talking about

There is more that can be added to this amount.
The book for demons you must have read it
and if you didn't don't! But don't say you won't
Because we need to understand evil in order to have hope.

The Poet Amin Speech

I want to tell you a story about a boy who couldn't read
He was always zoning out and was surrounded by greed
Every road was like a dead-end, and he had enemies for friends
So he kept a devilish grin, but wasn't ready for a life of sin
This story gets worse, the neighborhood was cursed
It was like a balloon burst

Watching children drink alcohol to quench their thirst
Drugs had us all wanting to be driven off in a hearse
And see who can meet the devil first
In time I became an outlaw eating heifers and hogs raw
And when they are gone I want more
because I am a human carnivore

People of this world can be real mean
Like a beast man officer riding around with a gangster lean
Thinking every lost soul is a mobster
Boiling us alive in the pot of corrections like lobsters
Making the bubbling water even hotter
Once they discover what's inside his locker

Sending him straight to the doctor
That's when I'll break the world off something proper
With the light shining from inside my head
That accumulated from back when I was dead
One of the reasons this Poet take meds
Has a lot to do with some of the things I said

Which makes me feel useless at times but my mind won't let me
Stop writing about this world's reality through the art of poetry
That has made life for me a little to conscious Holy
And you can ask anyone that truly knows me
How I be sharing information like a wise Liberian
Facing a day of judgment without properly preparing

Caught up within the game of truth while daring
To take control of this wheel that our Creator is steering
For a place upstairs inside the attic of our homes
Being revealed in some stranger's beautiful poem
Never grasping the facts about life until we prone dying alone
Swallowed by the Father of Death

Whose only promise to us was breath
But still remaining open to grow spiritually
Bringing a smile to mommy and daddy
Grateful for all the good company that's backing me
On the positive tip it's like being on a worldly trip
That I am holding onto with a tight grip

Enjoying this sweet cake mix that won't make you sick
But instead quite energize with realization for real lies
Darkening interpretation from interfering with the youth generation
Designed for them to keep celebrating with Satan
And believe me it hurts to see this plan work
Burying truth we need to know deep down in the dirt

But thank the Lord for all that was contemplated
Dropping seeds like I masturbated
As those who are wicked by nature will forever hate it
Living of a world that God created
But only the purified men will make it to a community so outdated
Trying to reach one of each student that will someday teach

Knowing that someone might be listening every time we speak
Swimming around in danger waters of the shadow creek
Fighting creatures of the deep by staying humble and meek
Hitting them with the heat of a wise man's words sort of speak
Watching them all weep whenever hearing the Poet Amin speech

Now That's Poetry

Everybody has an opinion, no one is sinning
The devil is winning overall with the laws
And that's the cause for us rebels not to find reasons to pause
But that's not it, more verses are being kicked
With common sense, humor and wit
Picture a painting of a beautiful waterfall. Now that's poetry

Some of my poems get stored, knowledge is poured
From out of my brain to be self-absorb
Reading Godly books has open up doors
Draw a butterfly; she's an angel of mine
Mother Almighty help create this rhyme
My soul has been in places where the sun doesn't shine

But even in the pouring rains I still write poetry
I figured out what's missing, and I know what's holding me
But I'll always be a master of the ceremony
Not only do I express worthiness
These poems were made to be impervious. Now that's poetry
I could end this but that would be too short

And I need more time to complete this fort
Because what I'm saying wasn't meant to be told in a code
It's something I feel the world needs like the oil being sold
Look at the two big stones blocking the dirt road. Now that's poetry
The little boy and girl walked in between
Birds chirping to connect my theme

She cried in the sunshine while he danced when it rained
Love and hate is one in the same
Holding on to guilt got me feeling ashamed
Death after life means surviving pain. Now that's poetry
There's always two sides to every story so hear them tell it
Because what I'm saying is meant to be pestilent

Twenty-one poems passed away
And ended up getting buried in a private cemetery
My job as an artist is to become spiritually richer
But for now I am getting paid as the gravedigger
and I get highly upset when families litter
Doing the butt sucking up squirrel nuts. Now that's poetry

Meditation has made me a better listener, if I could only go in deeper
It's time to start doing forget about trying
The serial killer was the Giant Lion
She sat next to me by the river helping with these poems I deliver.
Now that's poetry. There's a lot in the attic, but no light in the lamp
So I've come to disenchant because I'm very anent

and obviously blessed to be annuitant, but still attack an antagonist
or red, white and blue, that's why Mr. Evil be frightened
When I sound off boo!! Now that's poetry
My Father was a soldier and my Mother an outlaw
And I'm the comer of Light, but drugs were my downfall
Hearing her sweet voice throughout the song

Is what kept the art visualization flowing strong
And sometimes my love lasted all night long
I know for a fact that she will remember my name
I created poems to massage her brain
I'm from the land of the strange seeking change for the same
Not another person to place blame for causing me to go insane

Feeling nothing but guilt at the end of life or at the end of the game
Always wanting to drive in the fast lane to get to the core
or to the roots of my brain strain. Now that's poetry

Misdirection

As I walk through the tunnel of life
I shall inherit the courage to be brave my spirit will not fade
Accepting God's word for my soul to be saved
Dropping out of school in the tenth grade
If I was a straight A student I wouldn't have stayed
There were too many robots in my face

With beautiful smiles so heavenly grace
And after that the Poet disappeared without a trace
So much alcohol and drugs; my writings became a waste
Trapped by time and space forcing me to be a disgrace
So now I'm turning my mind into a solitude place
I spotted my kill in a big field refusing to serve the poor a meal

Seen as a god like an Egyptian Pharaoh
Communicating with Moses through talk radio
It was a miscommunication from all the static
So to hold my title I had to perform magic
And if I couldn't produce that would be my head
So I rose The Poet Amin up from the dead

Some plan to withstand what we have captured on cam
It's so unbelievable like a politician scam
I heard doors slam and the jelly jam
Like an eye for an eye or a foot for a hand
I'm turning into grease frying in a pan
Or a Vietnam Vet saying fuck Uncle Sam

Dangerous grounds have always been around
When one poem is lost, two poems are found
Hell's Fire decrease the works in my folder
Holding the weight of this world on my shoulders
After shock earthquakes killed my heart's hate
What I saw was final, destiny, and fate

Wondering how can a place so beautiful house a garden snake?
Opposite attracts I shouldn't have to remind you
That poetry is creative whether it is mindless or mindful
So why would someone want to stop light from shining through
I think it's time we search within to find this amazing creator
That keeps the universe vibrant like the satellite above the equator

Dust to ashes a falling star smashes like bombs be blasting
and at the same time someone is crying while others are laughing
This is a view of ugliness that I am giving to you
Because her kiss was deadly she gave me the flu
So after I kill her I plan to kill me too
Souls will swirl as men continue to destroy this world

I'm sending in troops to steal all your expensive pearls
A man's nice coat, a woman's pretty fur
But my goal is to be positive so forget everything you just heard
I want to be free and fly like a bird
Some of these suggestions are very absurd
So look, listen, try to feel and observe

because someone in the booth Is definitely keeping score
As I plan to do a song that you never heard before
The Poet's food needs to be cook well done
Competition's none, in 1987 my brother Keith was found hung
It blasted me, thrashed me, so fast I was stun
I still can't describe the pain in my mother's eyes

This is a time they took one of mine
He was ugly and beautiful, but not evil or divine
I hope he can see that I am stronger and no longer smoking crack
Every time I look up and see stars I remember how I used to see bats
My poems never lie they tell all the facts
But I've been released of blaming me because God has saved me

From the wicked witch who won't let me see my baby
Giving to you these visual impressions of a writer's perfection
Could this be a poet student guessing or a poet teacher testing?
And if you think it's all about me it has truly been a misdirection

Blowing In The Wind

I used to crawl around like a snake
But now I walk around like an ape
I'm a crime fighter when it comes to the cake
Or the Asiatic that wears the black cape
I need to do a little explaining before this poem starts changing
I was seen as a snake that rattles

I made this so called Adam eat the apple
and if you believe all the theories that the scientist make
before taking on this human form I was an ape
This is a story being performed on stage
For you all to feel the raft of the Poet's rage
They have most of our minds locked in a cage

Infecting the young with this disease called AIDS
Let me tell you about an innocent brother
He never knew because he had one lover
But she was HIV positive he got infected
Now they're both six feet under
I also hate the fact that drugs are being let in

Oh here I go switching it up again
But who do you think ends up in the pin
Tom Sawyer or Huckleberry Finn?
And why do you think God's people are paying for this
Because the founding fathers are Luciferins or atheist
I always wanted to come up fast

Never could learn anything in class
But that didn't last plus that was my past
So I won't be quitting just for the fact that I'm still living
And you can see that I have nothing but a lot has been giving
I also hope those serious about human services will improve
What the reformulation committee allow to be taught in schools

Because the rules of a fool are to work with their tools
So in the future you will lose, I suggest that you go to the library
Or the place where they bury the lies
And get that healthy Knowledge of Self by your side
So you can just walk on by
The demons with your head held high as the clouds in the sky

I can feel this cold wind blowing through city hospitals
Just for the fact that they all be killing people
And if you think what I just said despicable
That means these kind of situations are even more critical
It's going to be some kind of poisonous exploring
For the food that's in our stores, and

Soon when it gets down to the core, scientist will go on tour
Appearing to be astonishing so don't stop climbing the mountain
At least for the dead that's buried and rotten
Maybe gone but never forgotten entering the temple of doom
Smelling the gas fumes hoping not to hear the big bang boom
Creating characters to star in this life film of cartoons

Now is this all making sense because I know I'm not dense
And what this movement has become is an establishment
So let us continue with the fun
Preparing your minds for *A Night of the Sun*
Feeling like my brain weighs a ton
Deciphering through these organized writings

Listening while reading searching for meanings
Looking at poems can be like site seeing
The goal is to avoid negative traps and not taking part in evil acts
or any other senseless crap that leads to a forever resting nap
The wise will remain silent and hopefully not act in violence
It's all about receiving proper guidance

Because without that it will be about death and dead ends
Fighting wars that no one will ever win
Claiming that their dying for our sins
So we can commit them again
These thoughts are like leaves blowing wild in the heavy winds

Ranch of Jollies

The day felt peaceful as the sun shined down on the earth
And the Ranch of Jollies or poets and writers
Knowing that I'll be here on this planet earth temporarily
I need to enjoy every day of living, even when a love one dies
It is just another day of life, I see beautiful faces
Some look happy, some look sad, and some look confused

I have been writing words down on paper with my mind
Because both my hands have been chopped off
From taking things that didn't belong to me
Good thing I live in America
Where the punishment may be incarceration
Where you can still get an education

And be rebellious if you choose too
And suffer the consequences
of imprisoning your soul to closed mindedness
But my spirit is not imprisoned because I am free
And learning how to write with my feet
It takes patience and a lot of quality time

It used to hurt to see people mocking me
But that kind of ridicule is no longer stopping me
But maybe the man who cut down trees
Trying to destroy Mother Nature to make money
To support the blood baths of more innocent ones being killed
But all this evil cannot destroy my beautiful garden of flowers

Because love of knowledge equals mind power
Meanwhile back at the Ranch of Jollies
Poets wrote away with lots to say
I came with a blanket and on the pretty green grass I laid
My folders of poems come from planet starburst
or beautiful misses with sweet kisses

Walking down the street listening to music through my headphones
Seeing pretty faces, some happy, some sad, and some confused
With beautiful eyes, different shades of brown,
Blue, hazel, and green, for this I am grateful and full of life
It is like I never got up out of the bed today
And I am lying there hugging the pillow

But deep down in my heart I know it is really her
Because she dares not leave me, I pray every day

Day Dreaming

As my heart skips a beat I leaped into an ocean of love
I see her from a distance, I contemplate my move
Then I proceed to grab my family jewels
She has the prettiest smile and the wind's blowing her hair
And I just love those legs, hey I'm not scared
So I approach my friend, hi, how are you?

I'm on my way to a recovery barbecue
You want to come along? "No, because I'm busy
I'm on my way to the store for chili"
I probably would have been better off
Inviting her to a game of Frisbee
Well I guess the time and place wasn't meant to be

And hopefully I get to see her again eventually
Now when the moon is filled with the people we love
I'm still the sun and my Mother is the womb of the universe
Saying let Nature take its course
Sitting back scoping out the female anatomy
From all different nationalities gladly

But here she comes telling me no again
For some reason I just cannot seem to win her love
She will not budge and that's only because
Confusion can be excitingly amusing
Plus I didn't receive a smile when she accepted the flowers
It feels like my world is coming down like the twin towers

But I feel like I am in real needy for this particular sweetie
When I saw her wearing that yellow bikini
I started speaking in Swahili, as I envisioned her rubbing my leg
and asking me "what's the deally" and then I replied
I think it's about time for me and you to get freaky
And this may have been a large portion of lust

Because her loving is a mystery
Well at least that's how it seems to me
But I can't complain, the spiritual exercises were good
And if I can live forever with her in this bed I would
Now before we depart, it feels like she is going to break my heart
Because I'm like a big emotional board nailed to a wall

And she is poking me with darts
As I proceed to ask her, can I bring you lunch today?
And she said "You know I'm going to be busy"
Then I said how about breakfast at Tiffany's?
And I was picturing the sun setting as she put on them jeans
And then the doorbell ringed and messed up my day dream

Delusion of Self

The trees were all different colors like a rainbow
With bright colorful leaves falling down from them
The sun shined and water ran rapidly
Like my favorite stream out in the middle of the woods
Housing Cray fish, where I used to go and catch them
Walking through the trails reminiscing about the days of old

I started seeing myself surrounded by darkness
Sinking spiritually and living lonely filled with emptiness
Drinking the devil's booze and drugging, disrespect was at large
The dead leaves that were on the ground
Position themselves back onto the trees
The beautiful flowers of my poetry garden started looking ugly

Fruits and vegetables rotten and I was hurting inside
Trapped under pouring rains
Fighting my own demons on the battle field
But unsuccessful in winning locked back up behind bars
With all the so-called losers as the water in the stream stood still
And my heart was crushed as the grave diggers buried my body

In the poorest part of the cemetery, and that would be either side
of that house on Smally Street
But now that families been buying their loved one's tombstone
It could be considered somewhat special
Sleeping forever with the devil and his students
Because with the lack of love and true knowledge

Man becomes wicked and we start thinking
We were created different, no longer wanting peace
or having any room for happiness
So I have been working on rebuilding my faith
Letting sunshine enter into my mind
As the shadow of death begins vanishing

Flowers in the garden started blossoming again
The leaves on the trees are beautiful all over
The water in the stream never stopped flowing
Because God is good always
and the soul of our Mother's Nature will never die

I've Lost My Soul

My head is like a tennis ball and the world is a tennis racket
My world view of life has become foggy and very distracted
Being swung back and forth and still it is not enough
So a world living among the righteous has been calling my bluff
Because I just cannot resist the temptation of this savage beast
Knowing that a disturbed spirit will never rest in peace

I have really slipped and finally lost my soul
Now I am forever feeling lonely and cold, evil within has grown
And the devil has stripped me from out of all my clothes
Robbing me of my dreams as I walk around with my head low
Looking through the eyes of lust, not having any kind of trust
What little love I did have been gone since my spirit got crushed

Drowning in them dark waters that rushed up my body
Now I am feeling real sloppy because that crack cocaine rocked me
On my knees begging the Lord please have mercy upon my soul
Taking me away with ease and proven to be an incurable disease

Deadly Disease

I sat on the wall with Humpty Dumpty
And out of the blue he took his cigarette and burned me
So he and I got into a little squabble
He hit me so hard my brain wobbled
No I didn't lose because I woke up in the hospital
But they told me that they had brought me back from death

Like if that's really possible
Then I got mean like for the crack when I used to fiend
Because the police wanted me to write out the scene
Well early this morning my mother called me a junkie
So I went out in the jungle and had sex with a monkey
Then they all looked amazed

As they kept reading what I had wrote down on the page
Because now I carry this disease called AIDS
And it passes on like the Gods pass knowledge
Destroying poor communities and the minds of those in college
I was trapped in a hole six feet deep, feeling real weak
And some un-classy women had called me a creep

So I started climbing up to my highest peak
And other writers even acknowledged that my art was unique
Now I'm hungry seeking something to eat
I was thinking pig's intestines or pig's feet
I'd rather be in a casket having my body rot
Before I side or have a civilized conversation with any cop

But then I felt stupid crossing Dawson's Creek
Because Humpty Dumpty is still out on the streets
Giving me anxiety just from thinking
What's going to happen the next time we meet
As we both continue to sow what we reap
I am surrendering to this darkness by letting my conscious speak

Uncontrollably connecting thoughts slowly
Acting out in character defects a little more boldly
Releasing my pain in negative ways
Walking around in a state of confusion most of the day
and not really having anything good to say
It's like going up a snowy hill on skis

Confronting the battle of two me(s)
Deep within the mind trying to arrest this deadly disease

Powerful Prayer

I felt the light of Her wisdom entering my conscience
After what was guaranteed to be a brighter morning
So I thought only because of the love sign warning
But after a while things started getting boring
Once I realized it was me on life's stage performing
Right in the middle of the hell storming

Like some prostitute on the corner whoring for the dollar
You may have heard me hollering for help
As my brain continued to melt
Scooping real low to get higher burning in a wild fire
For living dangerous like a live wire and just going crazy
Believing what I am seeing is clear when it is really hazy

Especially when everybody is out to get you and acting shady
Not really enjoying this show while sitting in the back row
Thinking how I ran in the darkness through the cold white snow
Hoping someday I'll make it to the end of the rainbow
Because as of late I have been coming real close
With exquisite abominate mythos

No longer losing because I decided to change the things I was doing
After the awakening of spiritual thinking
I have been trying to draw it within this art creation
Witnessing soul peace through poetry excitement
Total union and the unfolding of enlightenment
Now the sun shines on a world of poetry that was once dark

It took God, recovery and not to mention a magnanimous heart
Even those I didn't know played a part
Because when I was on the path of destruction
Pointing the finger and blaming others for my stupidity
While on those streets playing, there was a unity of people praying
For me to share with you all the good that I was meant to do
Oh recovery has been just so special and beautiful.

A Brighter Day

Traveling upstream like a fish upon a star I made a wish
Now it is definitely an honor and privilege to be living like this
Because the place I left is definitely not going to be missed
There is nothing but pain, spiritual suffering, and guilt there
Now I am finally amongst people who truly care
Who else could have shown me a new way to live

Oh man this is so beautiful
I finally found people who were at where I was at
and also very happy now, ready and willing to help
"There is a better way" is what they all have told me
And sometimes those be the words that hold me
It is like we all have become stars shining bright

And refusing to lose this fight
So I stay in constant contact with God through prayer
Plus life is like driving a car and you must steer
In search of a road that never ends
All these feelings of happiness have just started to begin
Now the mind could be in control and I don't want to debate

But whatever is happening to me now feels great
And thanks to all of you who took time out and prayed
For when I was burning in hell and for my soul not to fade
My everyday life is like entering the pearly gates
As long as I keep away from that poisonous bait
Like a fish biting onto a hook getting pull out of its world

Now you are a memory and sounds of pain is what we heard
All the power from within is gone in the wind
And we can't even get a chance to do it again
So the question I'm asking myself now
Is there really a paradise for some on the other side?
And maybe it is, but for some still don't want to die

That's why I'm letting death out accepting things I cannot change
Like warring with myself to keep from testing them hell flames
Because destination's a fire pit, maybe even after life
For my soul if I don't change it for the better
So I have been holding onto God with a tight grip
Even when I am feeling like shit

Hoping that I never forget to pray
And remain embracing these brighter days

Today I'll Win

My mind is made up; I am refusing any kind of drugs today
Because the devil always wins but it won't win today
I mean it won't beat me or cheat me
I'm tired of letting the disease of addiction defeat me
So I will stay strong throughout the day mentally
That's the way it is, and that's how from here on out it is going to go

My Higher Power is in control and even the drug dealers will know
That I be going to 12 step meetings most days and nights
So I can remain vigilant and bright
Because if we don't give up we won't lose this fight

Not This Time

Right now I'm feeling a little anguished
Because I don't speak a proper language
And how some would consider my poems dangerous
When they are actually sweet like a Cinnamon Danish
Let's not worry about whose fruit's the freshest
And just welcome along the young and the restless

A Poet's junkyard may be in the midst
Analyzing what type of a mess the world is in
My heart went cold in the center of the heat
Just right after I was getting over the suicide leap
So I can float down the ocean's shadow water creek
And arrive where my life experiences can teach

Those individuals' society recognizes as the bad ones
By people who are not afraid to talk about the Lord
And then go and have sex with the nuns
I am planning to quit smoking because I started doing it for fun
and that lasted so very long I could have cancer in my lungs
The other day I could have dined with some cocaine lines

But I stopped, thought, and said not this time
Because I can see myself fiending and expressing evilness
Actively using at brisk crawling around in a snake pit
Like I have been poisonously bitten on thin ice sliding and slipping
Stuck in the mud and spiritually sinking
But when I awoke from this nightmare everything felt fine

So I looked in the mirror and said think God it was not this time
See drug addiction is so deep; it tries to kill me in my sleep
Like nasty bugs squashed sticking to the bottom of my feet
Because no addict's unique, anyone of us can be beat
When we used to live and live to use
Riding on the highway of life with the car in cruise

Working with the devil tools getting battered and bruised
Just like the minds of our children in these American schools
Standing behind enemy lines as victims of organized crime
Destroying what could have been days full of sunshine
Only if I choose to drink and drug today but not this time!

It Must Have Been Something You Said

Yeah I have been sitting back thinking of you
And also thinking about some of the stupid things I did
Let me swallow my pride and move away from here
It might be easier to say if I sat over there
Asking for guidance on how to go about reciting prayers
Life could be full of suffering while trying to cope one day at a time

With all that is going on in my head
Who wants war? It must have been something you said
The answer has to lie within or I don't know
I have been searching through these thoughts trying to create a flow
Because I don't really know what's keeping me here
Then the Goddess whispered in my ear "Come pray over here"

I know I can rise above
Experiencing a form of Higher Self Love
Listening to meditation music to get in tune
And become spiritually fit writing poetry to heal the sick
I went walking along on a floor that was wet
And I heard people laughing when I slipped

But I got up fast with the help of God
Trying to meditate for an hour a day shouldn't be a lifelong job
As I took a deep breath escaping that mess designed as a test
Following no beast on a quest
Once I discovered that the poetry carnival has a scary house
They rewrote the exorcist for you and your spouse

Hearing screams but I have my eyes on the bird
So I guess I wasn't listening to myself while writing these words
But the inner eye was seeing because it is very observant
So whatever you thought it was it probably wasn't
The nature of my soul has risen from the Goddess whisper
I can still remember the first time I kissed her

On the psychiatric ward holding the Poet's sword
And it was very much a blessing when the time occurred
Connecting my soul to the spiritual world
And I am still writing poetry with my eyes on the bird
Discovering that the poetry carnival has a roller coaster
Operating to make an artist heart grow hot or colder

But I need you to continue to stand by me
and embrace my love for the art of poetry
The mind has gotten stronger since I been turning things over
To this godly source, knowing in order to save others
I would have to save myself first
The earth will continue moving as the wind keeps blowing

Death is more than less and everybody is going
To an unknown place to man
That only a spiritual mind may overstand
All I want is to be able to hold this love in my hands
And spread it all across the world's beautiful land
Admitting that I kind of got scared

When she surprisingly hand cuffed me to the bed
But that was just a game for her to play with my head
Eating up all my love like sugar cookies
So I would guess her sweet tongue houses all the goodies
That describes the fate of a Poet visionary
Meditating in cemeteries, trying not to hurry along the edge

Wonder woman has trapped spider man in these human webs
Forever sleeping alone at night in the bed thinking
Of this harsh reality that our truth is in the process of escaping
Overseeing these picture painting creations
Being read by others even when after I am gone like in dead
Just note my goal was to know the ledge
That connects to something I must have thought you all said

Spit on My Grave

It is time for you to recognize the holy one
This truth will be revealed
In a future project entitled a *Night of the Sun*
Those who are afraid of the light will continue to wear shades
And everyone that fears to hear what is real
Would probably want to come and spit on my grave

But true lovers of poetry be licking their lips
Wanting more like if they were eating some lays potato chips
Some things that are broken cannot be fix
Warring within my own mind until I master it
This is a cup of healthy poetry so come have a sip
And stop getting high off of cat food mix with dog shit

Accepting false facts that the enemy can attack
This situation is outrageous and an irrational act
Creating a bigger mess domestically suppressed
Feeling clinically depressed suffering from pains in my chest
Moving more towards death it's like burning in a living hell I guess
Drugs are our master and we are their slaves

Causing crucial disasters while spiting on peoples' graves
Where lost souls float telling us words they spoke
To others like them searching for hope
Keeping away from the night sun trying to cope
All of what I am saying was written down on a note
Because his tongue went missing after life slit his throat

This incident was instigated by the spiritually broken
Hiding the truth about this knowledge they have stolen
The 12 concepts of evil followed by dangerous outcomes
Somebody should have told you that the girl was dumb
The ocean of ignorant bliss persuaded the waves in negative ways
From way across seas just to come and spit on my grave

Some said they did it unconsciously but I truly doubt it
People, places, and things all got rerouted
Because this bomb of confusion has just sounded off
Destroying the boss and the churches cross
So what they have in store is to keep all the poets' poor
And that's just the way it is once it surfaces upon the shores

While out in the dark forest I am hearing the Giant Lion roar
Trying to enter a world where there are no open doors
To the light of the stage so we all can get paid
But instead they choose to spit in our faces and on our graves

Cemetery Growl

Welcome to this stage show boys and girls
We are about to walk through a lively dead world
The reason for the liveliness is because it growled
The question I have been asking myself now is how
It was a demonic spirit but the Poet didn't fear it
And it has to be a reason why some are blessed to hear it

Well the akashic records are housing the proof that reveals this truth
In this world for the dead there is evil spirits running loose
These kinds of thoughts particular have been trapped inside my head
Got me caught up in this man-made world of human spider webs
And the leader that led misunderstood everything my poems said
But I've been warned by those who are righteous

Not to play with wicked spirits rather they are alive or dead
And also not start trouble with the luciferins by using magic of red
Once a person's mind is completely made up
It's going to be hard to stop you, *Alla qusam abbess equerondavo*
The demon entered his heart right when he was just planning to stop
Now his poor family believes he has been possessed by a rock

So we may need an upright person for some spiritual rehearsing
Don't believe that nonsense
Mr. Evil has no power to cast a curse, and
In the process of resurrection, this evil took a change of direction
And no religion will be mentioned for all the masses protection
Those that know better will continue to stay away

While them demons be on a mission impossible
Standing on shaky grounds suffering in the devil gods' hospital
But the Son of man heard everyone screams from miles
While everybody else went running because the Cemetery Growl

When The Wind Blows

When I awoke from an unconscious state of mind
I used to approach the day with happiness
But as the wind blows, thoughts change
And in some places around here the grass doesn't grow
Entering the zone of unknowing, swimming in a pool of sharks
Just drowning in misery every few seconds of this beautiful life

The wind is blowing and I am starting to feel a cool breeze
Coming from the spirit of forgiveness, wishing it wasn't me
That got lost in this life's forest, never seeing the outside picture
And that would be living drug free and enjoying life as others do
But instead I'm traveling through these triple stages of darkness
With my head down, broken heart, and a blurry vision

Good thing the sun still shine in dark places
Providing Her with light to help me see
I never seem to have witnessed that before
I'm like the cold in Alaska freezing up and melting away like ice
As this stream continues to flow, around I went, and around I go
As the wind blows traveling fast as light, but the process is still slow

To the point that I really don't feel like trying anymore
Fighting the hesitation without concentrating
Maybe because at a young age I handicapped my thinking
I wish I could go back to the beginning and start all over again
Refusing to let my weaknesses win me over
Yeah it's been time to take a stand so where is the enlightener?

I want to experience true happiness before I die
So I flew across seas to try to put my mind at ease
But I can't seem to stop tossing and turning when it's time for rest
Especially when I'm depressed gasping for breath
Before death there was life for everyone
But once we received knowledge of God we been doomed and done

At least that's what they taught us
As we became invisible, only spirits and conscious souls can see us
Voices of my shadow attack in my mind causing anxiety
Got me walking with my head down and teary eyed
The world gets quiet and cold hearted
As my sadness turns into anger

I approach the outer world blind folded, not seeing others' success
But seeing my Mother's face, and then family and friends
I have never been there to provide for them
Because of spinning most of my life
Trapped in the Giant Lion's forest of ignorance
Swimming in a pool of sharks being eaten and swallowed whole

Next was a drug infested street corner confronted with loneliness
All washed up in a world of misery, this just had to be my destiny
and I hate myself for it, so now I am seeking peace
And the right approach for a new start of the same beginning
Climbing up through the clouds holding onto pieces of air
Then a strong wind comes blowing moving me back over here

See every step I take I can feel the strong winds blowing
and the Poet isn't always prepared, thoughts of the weak-minded
But I'm not going to even take it there
Mother's beautiful Nature is within all of us
and there is always someone who cares
So now I try to walk with my head held high

But my feet still feel tied together
Trying to stop me from making my life better
Knowing that I need to take time out to pray throughout the day
Because I worked very hard for this, and I never have time to play
Man and Woman came together, if not none of us would be here
Picture a world of emptiness performing on stage with no one there

Seeing everything as everything, like the sharks of her beautiful sea
It's survival of the fittest, like human beings eating meat, one day
I will return back to dust, and the wind will blow on without me
That's one of the main reasons, I wanted to leave behind book copies
Expressing my visions and philosophy, needing no one to agree
Because many years ago, those yet born are going to have to know

About a captain of the poets, who had the most creative rhyme flow
And even after his death, you can feel it when the wind blows

Destination's Final

Hi everyone and welcome aboard
I hope you all have enjoyed every aisle of this candy store
Freshly picked fruits and vegetable soup
As I try to make this ball of knowledge inside the hoop
For whatever it costs trying to empress the boss
With amazing architecture just showing off a little bit

As if there is really some good in it
And that's not a question or trick, so feel free to think quick
Wiping off the lint and recognizing the hint
In today's lecture of arithmetics'
A positive role model describing an American idol
That you may even be able to hear on vinyl

For future titles about the contribution recitals
But these words are final
With a better description that was written by poets on a mission
And that in itself is like a benediction
Because what was missing was learning while listening
To others share their lessons on strengthening

Communities as a whole with a heart of gold
Before them devilish systems take control
On an individual basis selling our souls into a world that's cold
Watching everything unfold from a story one told
Which I thought was very bold on their part
But the facts still remain no one can destroy God's art

Delivered as a gift, reality or myth
Hoping life would be missed if I was granted one wish
And acknowledgment as being the creator of a poetry twist
Taking it back to the streets
Amongst the so-called druggies and winos
Because it has to end where it started destination's final

The Holiness of God

Let's listen to our heart beats pumping
Then imagine it stopping all of a sudden
The mind's doing too much running
Through the darkest parts of this evil dungeon
But I know the power of God will continue to rub on me
And my beautiful Mother will always love me

So why did I choose to take the path
That was rough like a game of rugby?
I decided to eliminate the hating but remain devastating
Even though I never spoke hate
But this is the kind of poetry that may be my fate
Because the underworld bank links to them poetry tanks

With so much wisdom being produced from the thoughts we think
Now my head is above them dark waters like the sun rising
So when God expresses His Holiness don't let it be surprising
Just see the light shining from the mesmerizing
Other poets combining and spiritually thriving
Those filled with negativity will be running and hiding

Just moving out of our way
When they really should be trying to stay
And embrace these fresher mornings living in a brighter day
Because this soul takes flight with those that are upright
Like the stars shining above us at night
So whomever be the buyer know that God will take you higher

Than any particular writer or spiritual guider
Catching the ball God is throwing through a stream of words flowing
And universally growing like a statue glowing
In the middle of nowhere or in the land of unknowing
Avoiding petty self destructions with no technique constructions
Within different dimensional discussions of higher being productions

Being revealed in time
Traveling with Michael Orbit through deep space nine
Seeing close encounters of a third kind
As reason and rhyme enters our minds
From the very beginning this has been a sign
Of studying long becoming wiser and strong

Like if a person can really live a whole life
Without doing anything wrong
It's like working an everyday job
Trying to see within this thick cloudy ignorance of fog
Life is all about positive change and getting closer to God

About the Author

Tarik Clayton, a/ka/a "The Poet Amin", is a native of New Britain Connecticut. He owes his writing journey to his older brother Aaron who inspired him greatly. It all started in 1983 when he discovered Aaron's personal collection of rhymes, while snooping through his sock drawer. That day changed his life tremendously, and since then he has been creating his own rhymes.

The Poet Amin started a poetry reading at the New Britain Public Library, With The Hard Hittin' Poets in 2009. His goal was to expand regionally and it did. He hosted readings at Trinity on Main Performance Art Center, Community Central, and the New Britain Museum of American Art, also in New Britain.

The Poet Amin lives and breathes poetry and considers himself a visionary.